Post•View of
Bristol

Post•View of Bristol

EVENING POST

DAVID HARRISON
with Gerry Brooke

Breedon Books
Publishing Company
Derby

First published in Great Britain by
The Breedon Books Publishing Company Limited
Breedon House, 44 Friar Gate, Derby, DE1 1DA.
1998

ISBN 1 85983 121 4

Printed and bound by Butler & Tanner Ltd., Selwood Printing Works, Caxton
Road, Frome, Somerset.

Colour separations by Freelance Repro, Leicester.

Jackets printed by Lawrence-Allen, Avon.

Contents

Introduction

THE *Bristol Evening Post* was born on 18 April 1932, in the ashes of a once flourishing newspaper industry.

The city had been the home of a large number of newspapers, from the 18th-century *Postboy* and *Felix Farley's Journal* onwards.

By the 1920s, a full-scale newspaper war was under way as the *Evening World* — part of a chain with which Lord Rothermere hoped to blanket the regions — rapidly killed off all the Bristol papers, apart from the morning *Western Daily Press*.

A group of Bristol businessmen and civic leaders got together, bought second hand and discounted machinery and set up the rival *Evening Post* in an old leather warehouse in Silver Street.

In the end, as in every other English city, there simply wasn't room for two evening papers, and the *Evening World* vanished. The *Evening Post* also took over the ailing *Western Daily Press*.

In 1932, the Post inherited the library of the old *Bristol Times and Echo* and its predecessors. The *Evening World* library followed in the sixties, as did the archives of the *Western Daily Press*.

If all the pictures and negatives had been kept, it would have needed a library of books like this to show off even a fraction of them.

Sadly, many were simply thrown away in the constant search for space in the days before computerised storage. Others have just deteriorated over the years; still more were 'borrowed' by collectors and authors and never returned. Some have even surfaced openly in their own books and with dubious copyright claims. But at least the images survived.

Until the mid sixties, the majority of photographs were taken on plate cameras using fragile glass negatives. Glass negatives and big lenses could produce an image of a sharpness and clarity which eludes film even today.

The *Evening Post* still holds a big collection of glass negatives — some inherited from as far back as the 1860s, some taken by its own photographers over the past seven decades.

They have been carefully stored in a cool dark room where business records and archives are also kept safely. Out of sight and out of mind, too, for they have never been properly catalogued.

We knew there were some treasures hidden away in the dark. We never appreciated just how many until we started checking through the piles of boxes. You will find photographs in this book that you have seen before but there are many which have never been printed or which have remained untouched since their sole appearance in one of the Bristol newspapers, decades ago.

Our own archives have been enhanced immeasurably by readers anxious to share their own old photographs and postcards. We have included some of the best with gratitude to all who have contributed, but in particular to Maurice Bye of Westbury-on-Trym, Peter Davey of the Bristol Tram Photograph Collection, former Bristol sports and features writer Chris Ducker, Brian Drew from Brislington, and Lewis Wilshire of Hanham. There are no thanks for those who tried to sell us pictures originally taken by our own photographers!

This book covers about 100 years, from the mid Victorian era, through the Boer War and two world wars to the mid years of this dying century. We've concentrated on the early years — up to 1960 really — because that's where the strengths of the *Evening Post* collection lie and where the real surprises are.

Few of the pictures, especially those on glass negative, have retained their captions, which means our dating and identification has often been done by examining clothes styles, car models, faded street and shop signs — and, occasionally, pure guesswork. If we have got it wrong, forgive us — it hasn't been easy at times although computer technology, with its ability to magnify tiny sections of pictures, has helped us pin down previously unidentified photographs.

There are plenty left over and who knows — if you enjoy this one, there are more than enough for another volume.

David Harrison

Pre-World War One

BRISTOL in the Victorian era was a grimy disease-ridden city of narrow, insanitary streets, water-ways that were used as open sewers, and one of the worst national death rates from cholera.

The rich had long since abandoned central areas for the cleaner slopes of Kingsdown and Clifton and left the city to the new industries — the railways, mills, glasshouses and great smoky factories.

It was a time when ships were beginning to abandon the Port of Bristol as they grew too large to sail the tidal Avon safely.

It was also an exciting time of innovation, new research, important inventions and great discoveries. There was certainly no sign of the sun ever setting on the Empire, and Bristol was at the heart of Empire trade.

Rail and canal linked it with the rest of the country but it remained a tight urban area surrounded by some of the best countryside in Britain. Brislington was still a beautiful village: so, too were Clifton, Westbury-on-Trym, Henbury, Henleaze, Horfield and others which have now been swallowed up by the city.

As the Victorian era drew to a close, Bristol cannily combined celebrations for Victoria's 60th year on the throne with the building of a tower to mark the 400th anniversary of John Cabot's journey to the New World.

Clifton Suspension Bridge was illuminated with 3,000 lamps — quite a task in those days — and a new dock started at Avonmouth. There were more paupers in Bristol than any other British city, yet 17 new churches and 14 mission halls were being planned.

A gift from tobacco baron Sir W.H. Wills helped launch the city's art gallery collection and the much admired Colston Hall burned down. The city gained new public baths, its first underground public convenience, electric trams, and a museum and reference library, and Bristol's mayor became a Lord Mayor to mark Victoria's birthday.

The Gloucestershire regiment set off for the Boer War and a new Colston Hall was built. And Bristol began to lose the open river in the centre which was once its best known feature.

It was a time of expansion and prosperity for some and grinding poverty for others, and it ended, together with the lives of so many young Bristolians when a local conflict in the Balkans flared into a terrible world war.

The day after the disastrous fire that wrecked Bristol's Colston Hall in 1898. It started in a wholesale clothier next door and quickly spread into the Colston Hall roof. The great hall and famous organ was completely destroyed.

The Colston Hall after the 1898 fire, showing the remains of the elegant interior and the pillars which must have blocked the view for a lot of the audience.

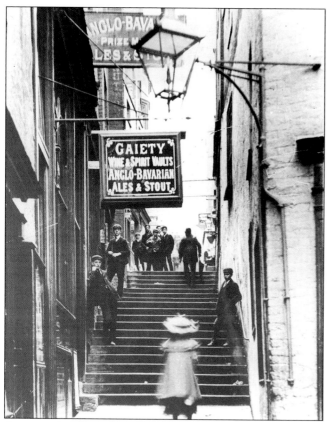

An evocative shot of the famous Christmas Steps around the turn of the century. Note the Anglo-Bavarian beers on sale at the Gaiety wine and spirit vaults which puts this before World War One. Presumably the loungers were fascinated by the camera rather than waiting to waylay the little girl.

A crowded Christmas Steps in the Edwardian era with straw boaters mixing with flat caps This is one part of ancient Bristol that has survived, virtually unchanged apart from the signs. The city beyond is very different.

Evidence that the great engineer, Isambard Kingdom Brunel, was not always right! This was taken in the 1870s and shows workmen at Temple Meads replacing Brunel's much vaunted broad gauge lines with the standard gauge used by most of the rest of the country. In the background is the Bristol and Exeter railway building.

An 0-6-0 saddle tank on the highly eccentric Weston, Clevedon and Portishead Light Railway. The company bought just two new locomotives in its 42 years of existence — the rest were picked up cheap from other railways, resulting in the most varied fleet in Britain.

Carriages on the Weston, Clevedon and Portishead Light Railway were as curious as the locomotives. Some were originally intended for a South American railway, others were bought from British companies. Getting in was no easy matter at some stations.

A lone passenger in plus-fours and baggy mac waits for a Weston, Clevedon and Portishead Light Railway service. Locals loved to advise visitors to go on the WC and P!

West Street, Bedminster, around the turn of the century. Note the by-products of horse transport all over the road. This was the main thoroughfare into Bristol for carriers from the agricultural areas to the south.

This looks like an advertising photograph for A.C.Haskins, baker and confectioner of 183/185 North Street, Bedminster, who is obviously enjoying showing off his smart horse-drawn delivery vans.

Assembly line, Wills style. Hundreds of women and girls pause for a moment from cigar making to smile for the camera in the factory where they were guaranteed a job for life. It was the place everyone wanted to work.

The workers of the Capper Pass smelter in East Street, Bedminster, where lead reclaimed from old Roman and Medieval workings on Mendip was re-smelted using the latest Victorian technology. They were pictured in 1887.

A loaded timber carriage pulled by three horses, waiting to unload at Toogood's timber yard, West Street. Opposite is Wintle and Sutton, grocer, on the corner of Bartletts Road.

The White Hart in Broad Street with the White Lion next door. The notice on the side of the Hart reads: 'Post horses, Private Pair and One Horse Carriages Welcome.' Both inns were demolished in the 1860s to make way for a new White Lion, which was eventually renamed The Grand Hotel.

Looking up Broad Street towards the Dutch House in the Edwardian years. The people on the right are waiting for the quarter jacks outside Christ Church to sound bells to mark the quarter hour. On the left is Rippon Bros' hosiery shop and Hunter and Vaughan, gunmakers and athletic outfitters.

Chamberlain Pole and Company's offices in Lower Union Street. The company sold Rapid Growth Poultry and Chick Foods, as advertised on the top of the building.

Union Street with the old meat market on the right where the Galleries shopping centre now stands.

Mother and children on Ladies Mile on The Downs in the last days of the Edwardian era. Notice the little boy's horse on wheels and the elegant clocktower-topped pavilion in the background.

Tram service across the Downs, just before World War One.

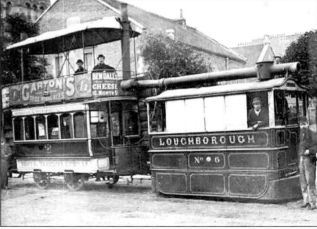

This amazing contraption is an experimental steam tram which ran on the Horfield line for a short time in 1880-81. It actually had a roof which was unusual (and popular), but residents and traders complained of the noise and smell and they were withdrawn after a year.

An incredibly well-stocked Halford's cycle shop in Bristol in 1910. This was probably taken for an advertisement as all the staff are posing outside.

Another very early photograph showing the uncomfortable horse trams that Bristol Tramways ran from 1875 until the turn of the century when the city was one of the first to introduce electric trams. These contraptions could carry 32 passengers but were often loaded with twice as many. Pity the poor horses.

An evocative picture of ships moored deep in the heart of Bristol in around 1870 with St Stephen's and three other churches in the background.

St Augustine's Bridge crosses the centre where the old drawbridge used to stand. Familiar names like Husbands and Dunscombes were already established near the Hippodrome on the left, with Werner, Pfleiderer and Perkins who made kneading and mixing machinery, on the corner of Colston Street.

Sailing ships at the Drawbridge on Bristol Centre, one of the most evocative views of the past which drew admiring comments from every visitor. In the background is Taylor's, wholesale leather exporter.

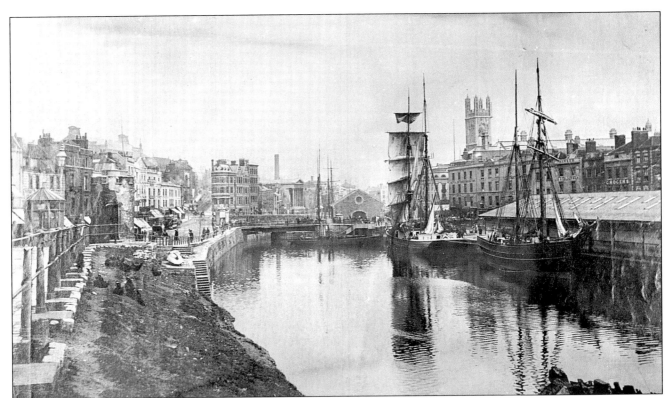

The Centre in Bristol in the days when sailing ships could moor in the heart of the city. This was probably taken in the 1880s before the Drawbridge became a fixed bridge and the upper harbour was closed in, and when St Mary-on-the-Quay church really was on the quay.

The Centre in 1895 with horse taxis waiting and not a car in sight. This scene is not too different today, although some of the buildings have been replaced and the river to the right is now covered by gardens.

Another view of The Centre in the days when it was still open to sailing ships.

The end of King Street with the Llandoger Tavern (now the Llandoger Trow) on the right and the Old Duke (then the Duke of Wellington rather than the Duke Ellington as now, of course) to the left. The Llandoger, built in 1664, lost the two end gables in an air raid of 1940.

The original entrance to the Theatre Royal in King Street — otherwise known as the Old Gaff music hall. The splendid building to the right of the picture is Cooper's Hall, now incorporated in the theatre complex as the box office and reception area. The old houses were demolished in 1903.

The Round House, an old toll house which survives today, at Ashton Gate. It was converted into old people's homes in the seventies.

Laying electric cables in the 1890s in High Street. Note the posters for the Theatre Royal and Princes Theatre on the walls of the boot shop. Bridge Street can just be seen in the background.

Looking down High Street to Bristol Bridge and advertisements for Veno's Cough Syrup and Dr Cassell's Tablets on the buildings in Victoria Street. To the left is the City Bible Warehouse and W.E.Robertson, tobacconist.

Looking up High Street from Bristol Bridge with Back of Bridge Street and Bridge Street to the right and Baldwin Street to the left. None of the buildings on the right survived the Blitz.

Brislington village with N.J.West, painter and undertaker on the right and a tobacconist's shop to the left. Brislington was then a quiet Somerset village on the road to Bath.

The art gallery in Queens Road with electric trams outside, around the turn of the century.

Whiteladies Road, named after the white habited nuns who lived on the site of the current cinema. Neither this name nor that of Blackboy Hill have anything to do with the slave trade, as visitors presume. The Alexandra Drapery Company is on the right.

Blackboy Hill, Clifton with a mixture of tram lines and horse droppings covering the road. The tram lines are separated by wooden blocks. On the right is James Highnam, artists' colour-man and picture frame makers.

It's a very familiar picture but it belongs in any picture book of old Bristol. This is Fred Little's famous shot of the old Black Boy Inn which gave the hill its name. To the left is another pub, the British Workman. The Inn was demolished for road widening.

An unusual view of Park Street in 1900 from College Green. Businesses on the right at this time included the Cathedral Temperance Hotel, a Post Office, G.M.Halfyard and Brownlow, both costumiers; Liberty and Co, William Roberts and Co, tailors; and London Rubber Company.

The Kings Arms pub on Blackboy Hill. The building is still there but without the elegance and style it once had.

Queens Road in the Edwardian era, viewed from outside the Victoria Rooms. On the right the headquarters and warehouse of shoemakers Lennards, with the Boer War memorial in front of the tram. Apart from road alterations much of this scene is little changed today.

Mystery shot. This is one of a series believed to be in a girls' school in Clifton, but where and when isn't known. It was obviously May if the maypole dancing was in season and warm enough to sit on the grass.

A wonderful Edwardian photograph of Wine Street, once part of the biggest shopping centre in the West. On the right is the Domestic Bazaar Company, Lewis Protheroe, photographer, and Henry Samuel, watchmaker. On the left is The Don, selling boys' school and college outfits; Baker Baker, Home and Colonial, and Jones and Co.

The linen draper's shop at 9 Wine Street above which poet Robert Southey was born in 1774. The building was blitzed and replaced by office blocks, including one named Southey House.

Wine Street, complete with street water pump, in the last century with three of the many inner city churches. A.Cameron on the right was a chemist, while Jones and Co on the left were linen drapers and house furnishers.

The little village of Whitchurch, long before it was surrounded by new estates. The building on the right is advertising a curious mix of tyres and Fry's Cocoa.

Stokes Croft with City Road leading off to the right. The building at the junction is Charles Clements, tailor.

The apple woman of Peter Street, a fondly remembered figure in a street that disappeared in the Blitz. She sat outside Melhuish's restaurant and her mother had the dubious honour of being the first to be winched across the Avon Gorge in a basket.

The junction of Peter Street and Castle Street in the heart of the old shopping centre. Garlick's Hats is on the right, with a special offer on fancy waistcoats, and Marks and Spencer's Penny Bazaar and W.H.Vowles, brush and basket makers, on the left.

This is Peter Street, another of the tightly packed little streets that made up Bristol's main shopping centre. It all vanished in the Blitz.

Old Market, with the premises of Frederick Sage, cork shive and spile maker on the right. A shive was a flat cork for a wide-mouthed bottle and a spile was a wooden peg driven into a beer barrel to allow carbon dioxide to escape during secondary fermentation.

Old Market is now little more than a busy through road, but in this picture it was still a thriving shopping centre where all the trams from east Bristol terminated. There was the Empire Theatre, Central Hall and, later, the Kings cinema, with the Castle Street area close by.

The suburb of Lawrence Hill with St Lawrence's Church looming over the street. The Glasshouse Hotel is on the right with an Anglo Ales poster on the side, and scalemaker C.W.Cook was next door.

The St Thomas area, viewed from St Mary Redcliffe tower. To the left, ships are moored along Welsh Back with the extraordinary Granary in the background. In front are factories, mills and back-to-back housing, little of which survives today. The road at the bottom right is Redcliff Street.

A traction engine turns into Redcliffe Hill with the tower of St Mary Redcliffe in the background. These steam driven monsters were once a common sight, pulling heavy loads through the streets.

Hotwell Road when it was a busy shopping centre around 1915. Businesses visible include F.Bennett, tailor, H.Evans, tobacconist and Albert Sweetman, family butcher and a telephone call office (all on the left) with G.E.Wright, pork butcher and bacon curer, and Lennards shoe shop on the right.

Right: Sober, dignified, eminently trustworthy – who could resist investing their hard earned savings with the gentlemen of the Bristol and West Building Society, pictured here in 1900.

Below: Merchant Street in the floods which swept through the area in 1882. On the left is The Standard Pure Bread and Flour Company and the Portrait Rooms, operated by photographer Walter Moore. Across the waterlogged street was the Pure Sweet Supply Company, R.D.Rickman, carpenter, plumber, painter and general builder, and Coombs and Co who were ticket and sign writers.

The Western Daily Press offices and printing works in Baldwin Street. The building survived the Blitz but was later demolished.

A tram moves carefully through flooding in Cheltenham Road in 1914.

High Street, Staple Hill, in 1900.

The Zetland Road junction in 1914 after floods had forced up the wooden blocks laid between the tram lines.

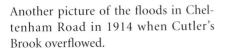

Another picture of the floods in Cheltenham Road in 1914 when Cutler's Brook overflowed.

The Pithay in 1890, seven years before the old houses were swept away for an extension to Fry's chocolate factory. Businesses at the time included Mrs Bell, grocer; Thos J.Gardiner, planemaker; James Welsh, greengrocer; Thomas Watkins, grocer, The Prince of Wales and Friendship pubs, and Christ Church Mission Room.

Crowds gather for the opening of the Edward VII Memorial Hospital – an extension to Bristol Royal Infirmary – by George V in 1912.

The Pithay, with Thomas Gardner, planemakers and toolmakers on the right and the Christ Church Mission Room and The Friendship pub to the left. This picture was also taken in the 1890s.

This row of houses was demolished to make way for the new Edward VII Memorial Hospital.

George V calls at the old Bristol Council House in Corn Street to knight the Lord Mayor after opening the Edward VII Memorial Hospital.

Floods in Broadmead in 1882 with wagon drivers making a nice little earner by carrying people through the water. Three inches of rain fell in less than 48 hours, many central areas were deep under water and a baker and his horse were swept away by the torrent and drowned.

A Campbell's White Funnel paddle steamer turns in Cumberland basin, ready to take a load of passengers for a day trip into the Bristol Channel.

Lewins Mead in 1907 at a show of dray horses, the heavy duty animals that pulled amazing loads through the streets of Bristol. The constable on the right was named Robinett. He became a sergeant before retiring to Fishponds. Few of the buildings survive today.

Bristol's elegant Corn Exchange just before World War One. The two carts outside belong to the Old Post Office Tea Warehouse.

Two views of the Lily Pond at Kingsweston House, in the early years of the century. Left shows the stables which still stand today.

Orphan boys outside the Muller's home on Ashley Down. They are all dressed identically in shirts with white turn down collars, high waistcoats, matching jackets, rough trousers and very short cropped hair.

A wonderful portrait of Old Market around the time of World War One when it was the main tram terminus for the east of the city. To the left is the Empire variety theatre where a young Cary Grant (then Archie Leach) had his first break in showbiz as a limelighter, and dozens of big and little shops including a bacon curer, dental surgery, and barber.

The funeral cortège of Private Thomas Bowen of Hotwells, a soldier with the 12th Battalion The Gloucestershire Regiment (Bristol's Own) for the shortest time on record. He volunteered in February 1915, collapsed on parade at White City, Ashton, on the 18th and died on the 21st. He was buried with full military honours in Arnos Vale. This picture was taken in Victoria Street.

Bristol Football Club (which confusingly played rugby) First XV in 1907-08. Captain was Harry Shewring (holding the ball) who played ten times for England and M.E.Kneale (to his left in the picture) was also capped while playing for Blackheath.

A rare picture of the immortal W.G.Grace practising in the nets. The Downend doctor is still considered as one of the greatest cricketers of all time and was instrumental in the opening of the County Ground in Bristol. He captained Gloucestershire for many seasons.

W.G.Grace at the wicket (in black shoes!). He was also a footballer, rugby player, huntsman and, above all, an athlete of considerable talent. Many Bristol sports meetings were dominated by Grace who hated to lose almost as much as he detested being declared out at cricket.

Edward, eldest of the four cricketing Graces. He was nicknamed 'The Coroner' because he was one (for West Gloucestershire) off the field. He played first-class cricket from 1861 and took part in the 1862 tour to Australia.

Walter Pearce of Bristol Football Club, pictured in his younger days. He played for Gloucestershire but was better known as club secretary for 14 years. He later became president of the Rugby Union.

Gloucestershire fast bowler Fred Roberts obviously posing for the camera. He was a left-hand bowler with a high delivery who in his later years became landlord of the Old England pub in Montpellier.

Not a bunch of Keystone Cop jailbirds, but Clifton Rugby Club team of 1876. The club was formed long before Bristol and was for many years one of the best in Britain.

Gilbert Jessop, known as The Croucher on account of his stance at the wicket, played for Gloucestershire 345 times between 1894 and 1914. He was renowned for rapid scoring and brilliant fielding, although his first England cap was as a fast bowler. He died in 1955 aged 81.

Bristol Rovers supporters look very gloomy at half-time in a Cup match with Portsmouth on 18 January 1912 – Pompey were leading 1-0. Someone at the rear of the picture on the left is holding up a pair of bloomers – a comment on the match? Less than half a dozen women can be seen among the crowds.

Laundresses at the Beaufort War Hospital in Fishponds take a break from what must have been very heavy labours to pose stiffly for the camera. This was part of a series showing how ordinary folk at home could help the war effort.

Left: The huge Dutch House on the Corner of Wine Street and High Street, another sad loss in the Blitz. Its origin is uncertain – it was either a genuine house shipped over in sections from the Netherlands or a replica – but it was one of Bristol's most distinctive buildings. This photograph was taken in 1884.

This fine tin soldier once guarded the first floor balcony on the Dutch House. He still survives today in the City Museum.

This is quaint Mary-le-Port Street, part of Bristol's famous central shopping area until German bombers levelled it. In the background is the tower of St Peter's Church which, unlike the shops and houses, still stands.

A little touch of Venice in the Avon Gorge. This eccentric building was a pumping station built by Merchant Venturers to supply quality spring water to Clifton and given an Italian look because of its sensitive setting. This photograph was taken in the 1850s and the station was demolished in the 1920s to make way for the new Portway.

A ship lies helpless on the mudbanks of the Avon in 1854. The fierce tides and winding course of the river brought many ships to grief and ended Bristol's pre-eminence as Britain's second most important port. It also led to new docks being built at Avonmouth and Portishead in an attempt to retain trade.

Allen's Angel Inn in Nicholas Street. with steps leading down to Baldwin Street between the pub and St Nicholas's Church. The inn is still a pub, the church has become the city tourist centre.

This narrow road with its bow fronted windows is believed to be Alderskey Lane, off Narrow Quay. Why anyone would want to photograph it isn't clear, but it has long since disappeared.

This picturesque old hostelry is the Rose and Crown at 38 Broadmead, which sold Ashton Gate beers. Proprietor was S.Harris. Next door is Thomas and Wagg which sold furnishing fabrics and trimmings.

The village blacksmith and some of his tools. This was John Foxford Radford who operated Radford's Shoeing and Smith's Forge in Westbury-on-Trym. The picture was taken in the 1890s.

Dial Cottage, Westbury-on-Trym, a former toll house for a packhorse bridge, which has an inset clockface on one wall. Legend had it that it always stood at 11.50, the exact time the spinster owner was jilted by her lover. This lovely shot featuring the local postman disappointingly shows it at 9 o'clock!

The tram terminus at Westbury-on-Trym, with Mogford's store to the left and the Foresters Arms pub behind the drinking fountain. Note the chap in the top hat on the open upper deck of the tram.

A rare picture of trams, taxis and new fangled motor buses waiting at the bottom of Temple Meads incline for passengers from the Great Western Railway.

The Higher Grade Technical school at St George, built 1894 at a cost of £14,000, which later became St George's Grammar School. It taught boys and girls together from its inception, a rarity in those days.

Jubilant citizens parade through the streets of Bristol in 1900 to mark the Relief of Mafeking during the Boer War. Streets were decorated, bells rung and hundreds of people joined the celebratory march.

Troops in Imperial pith helmets, Tropical Climes For The Protection From, join in the Mafeking celebrations in Bristol.

One of the famous Blue Taxis – registration number AE 1834 – draws up outside the Grand Spa Hotel in Clifton with the Suspension Bridge in the background. As the car had a number plate, the picture must have been taken after 1903 when they were first introduced.

Dockers at Avonmouth, just before World War One.

Avonmouth dockers pose for the camera in 1912. They had obviously been on a march as they have a flag and a band with them. On the left is a surgery, then owned by a Dr Rolfe.

Rysbrack's world famous statue of King William III in Queen Square in the days when it was protected by elegant railings and gas lights. This was long before a road was driven through the square in 1937. Notice the little girl at the right with the whip for her top.

A very rare photograph of the Cabot Tower nearing completion in 1898. The original is owned by Mr John Woods whose grandfather, Henry Horseman (standing, lower right), was foreman for building contractor Love and Waite of St Paul's. The tower was started in 1897 and cost £3,800.

These three images are of a Victorian amateur production of Gilbert and Sullivan's *The Mikado* in Bristol. They survive on mounted cards – and that's all that's known about them.

Old Church Road in Clevedon, another popular outing for Victorian families. On the right is the old cinema, showing a film called Beauty and the Badge.

One of the earliest photographs in this book. This is the old turnpike at Stapleton, some time after the middle of the last century.

Birnbeck Pier, Weston-super-Mare, built 1863 and a favourite day out for generations of Bristolians. The signs advertise a switchback and there were other fairground rides, a theatre, and cinema among other attractions. The building to the left – just before a giant sign advertising that only Impenetrable Paint is used on the pier – is the lifeboat house.

Court Lodge, Frenchay in a quieter, more idyllic era.

College Hill with the old Royal Hotel looming over the church of St Augustine the Less. The church was bombed and the remains demolished to make way for an extension to the hotel (now the Swallow Royal).

A view down the chains of the Clifton Suspension Bridge when it was being completed in 1864. Brunel, its designer, never saw it completed and his design was heavily modified to cut costs.

A truly historic photograph of the Clifton Suspension Bridge being built in the early 1860s. By this stage, the towers had not been topped off and the roadway is still unfinished. Sadly, the sphinxes Brunel wanted on top of the towers were never added.

Another picture of The Centre in the days before cars. Trams, horse taxis and carts make for a busy scene with the Colston hall looming in the background above Werner, Pfleiderer and Perkins who sold kneading and mixing machines.

The Elephant Inn, Nicholas Street, early this century. The pub still exists today.

A wintry scene in old Avonmouth.

The smart Continental Hotel in Avonmouth, around the turn of the century.

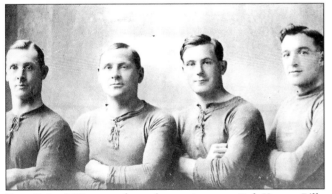

Four Bristol City stars from the great years – Bob Young, Billy (Fatty) Wedlock, the India Rubber Man; Laurie Banfield and Jock Nicholson.

Workers at the famous Lysaghts wire works in St Philips. This stiffly-posed picture comes from the Edwardian years.

These are the Blue Maids, orphans in a Bristol home which was founded in 1794 and closed in 1927. The home at Hook's Mill was noted for being well run and the girls happy.

World War One

REGIMENTS connected with Bristol were at the forefront of the conflict throughout. The 1st Glosters were in the original Expeditionary Force that gained the title of The Old Contemptibles – a casual jibe by the Kaiser which became a badge of pride.

The 2nd Glosters were in China when war was declared then served in the unimaginable killing fields of France and Belgium before transferring to Macedonia and the Salonika campaign.

There were the 12th Glosters, a Territorial unit raised by Bristol Citizens Recruiting Committee; the 4th (City of Bristol), the 6th of St Michael's Hill, the 14th (West of England Bantams), and other battalions of the regiment.

Many Bristolians also served in the Worcesters and Warwicks, the Royal Artillery, the cavalry of the Line, the Royal Gloucestershire Hussars, the North Somerset Yeomanry, Tank Corps, Machine Gun Corps and a number of South Midlands units. Many others were in the Navy, Royal Naval Reserve and Royal Flying Corps (later the Royal Air Force) but only army photographs seem to have survived in the archives the *Evening Post* inherited.

Volunteers for the 12th Glosters receiving rifle instruction at Ashton Gate in 1914.

The bizarre and rather poignant sight of war wounded soldiers taking part in races on crutches at the Beaufort War Hospital in 1916. The hospital, at Fishponds, was the former Bristol Asylum and is now Glenside Hospital.

B Company of the 12th Glosters march through Bristol in 1914.

Wounded soldiers at a Christmas dinner at the 4th Glosters headquarters in the Drill Hall, Old Market. The signs on the tables denote at which hospital they were being treated.

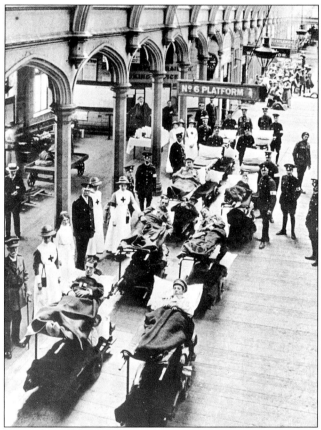

Wounded soldiers on stretchers at Temple Meads Station, waiting for ambulances to take them to hospital.

A company of Bristol's Own Battalion, The Gloucestershire Regiment, returning from rifle drill in 1914. They were training at the White City International Exhibition site at Ashton Gate which closed when war was declared and was then used as HQ by Bristol's Own.

YOUR KING AND COUNTRY NEED YOU

THE
NEW BRISTOL BATTALION GLOUCESTERSHIRE REGIMENT

To the Mercantile and Professional Men of the City of Bristol and Neighbourhood.

Lord Kitchener has sanctioned the enrolment of Single and Married Men of the City of Bristol and Neighbourhood between the ages of 19 and 35, who are willing to join the Colours for the duration of the War. The Battalion is to be a Battalion of Mercantile and Professional young men, under Officers of the Regular Army.

CONDITIONS:—

Married men are eligible and get separation allowance.

You must be between the ages of 19 and 35.
You agree to serve for the period the war lasts.
You agree to serve at Home or Abroad as may be required.
Clothing and Equipment will be supplied free by the Government.
Full Army pay.
The Battalion is to be an Infantry one, and will constitute a unit of the Regular Army.
Seven days' notice of calling up will be given.

If you wish to serve your Country in this time of stress, obtain the necessary application form at the New Battalion Offices, Colston Hall, Bristol, or any of the Bristol Banks, fill same in and send to

THE CHAIRMAN,
Bristol Citizens' Recruiting Committee,
New Battalion,
Colston Hall, BRISTOL.

AN APPEAL TO EX-N.C.O'S.

LORD KITCHENER appeals to Ex-Non-Commissioned Officers of any branch of His Majesty's forces to assist him now by re-enlisting at once for the duration of the war.

PARTICULARS.

Chiefly required to act as drill instructors. Promotion to non-commissioned rank immediately after enlist_ ment. Age no obstacle so so long as competent. No liability for service abroad if over 45. Pensioners may draw their pensions in addition to pay of rank at Army rates.

Apply for information to
MAJOR CARR,
8, Colston Street.

GOD SAVE THE KING.

An advertisement calling on Bristolians to volunteer for the Front which appeared in local newspapers in September 1914.

Patients and staff at Bishop's Knoll Hospital, Stoke Bishop, pose for a souvenir photograph. Most of the casualties here were Australian, although there is only one bush hat in sight.

An ambulance train arrives at Temple Meads station where the walking wounded are lined up for refreshments while stretcher bearers prepare to remove the more serious cases. Note the row of stretchers along the platform wall.

Volunteers who made up Bristol's new battalion in full marching order at Cumberland Basin in 1915. More than a third were killed or injured in the first few days of the Battle of the Somme.

Cheery smiles for the camera at the Glosters mess hall in 1914. Few of the lads in this picture survived the next four years.

The noble art of trench digging Part One. Volunteers for Bristol's Own get digging in July 1914.

Helping the war effort. These are workers at the Motor Construction Works in Bristol during World War One when women took over jobs previously reserved for men. It caused real problems when the men returned and wanted their jobs back – and women didn't want to give up their new freedom.

No 6 Horse Gun Team of the Warwickshire Regiment at Ashton Gate barracks in January 1916.

Bristol members of the Royal Army Medical Corps in France in January 1916.

Canadian troops marching through Shirehampton Park in October 1914.

One of the more bizarre images of World War One – soldiers of the 6th Battalion The Gloucestershire Regiment on a hopping exercise in 1914.

The headquarters guard of the 6th Battalion The Gloucestershire Regiment. Note the very long rifles of the time.

Soldiers in training with the Glosters take a break for the camera on a route march across steep Dundry Hill in 1914.

New recruits for the Gloucestershire Regiment in 1914, few of whom survived more than a few weeks.

A wounded soldiers' motor run organised by Southmead Infirmary and Bristol Motorcyclists' War Committee, October 1914.

Private C.Bullock of the Somerset Light Infantry in 1914.

New recruits muster at the Bristol Coliseum in Park Row (now part of the University Gate office development) in 1914.

A contingent of the Black Watch marches to its billet at the Colston Hall in November 1914.

Bristol's Own dining room at their Bower Ashton headquarters.

Bristol recruits to the 3rd South Midland Field Ambulance Corps unloading the wounded at a field dressing station.

A 3rd South Midland Field Ambulance Corps emergency ambulance ready for France.

Officers of the Bristol Coliseum Training Corps pose in the long grass at Bower Ashton in August 1915.

The 3rd Glosters on parade at their headquarters in Whiteladies Road before leaving for the front in 1915.

The 3rd and 6th Glosters on parade in 1915.

A smile from men of the South Midland Field Ambulance Corps as they train in a country lane near Bristol.

Woodall's elegant furniture shop at 11 Bridge Street around 1938.

Hodder's corner shop in Bridge Street and the neighbouring Swan Hotel and Vaults were up for sale in this picture from around 1938. Notice the advertisements for Golden Grain, 'the tea for flavour and economy', Sandeman's Very Choice Old Port, and Hodder's own sausages. Next door in Mary-le-Port Street is Wil-Sam-Mor (short for William Samuel Morris), a well-known wallpaper and paint shop.

Stead and Simpson's elegant shoe shop on the corner of High Street and Mary-le-Port Street with Prince's Grill above. All this vanished in the war.

Looking down Castle Green towards the school.

Bristol Co-operative's new premises between Castle Street and Castle Green, under construction in 1929.

A wonderfully evocative image of cinema-going before the war when audiences expected live music from an orchestra or at least an organist as well as the films. This is the Regent Cinema in Castle Street, one of the city's top cinemas, with the spotlight on the organist.

The premises of R.Hill and Son, cutlers and toolers, at 16 Castle Street. Next door is the Manchester Clearing House which sold bankrupt stock. Another view that vanished in the war.

Bristol's pre-war shopping centre was very different to the modern replacement. This shot shows Castle Street with familiar names like Marks and Spencer, Woolworth, Brooks and Boots among other businesses that disappeared with their shops in the war.

Two of the familiar toastrack-style trams waiting in Lower Castle Street.

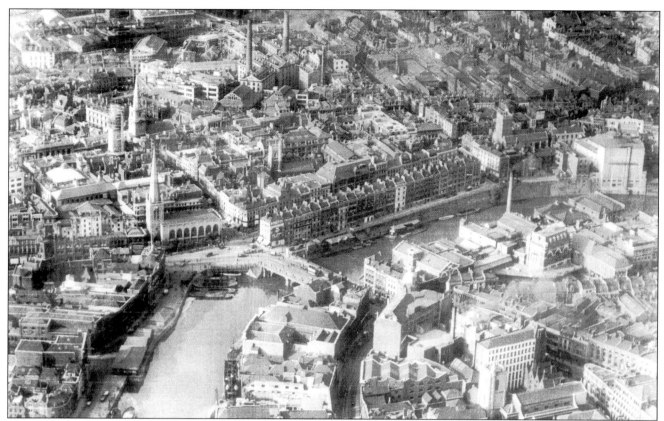

An invaluable aerial record of pre-war Bristol, showing how much has been lost. Bristol Bridge is in the centre, with the tall buildings of Bridge Street to the right and St Peter's church in the middle of a network of streets, shops, and homes which were largely destroyed. The tall chimneys at the upper centre are the old Fry's chocolate factory.

Castle Street, the most fondly remembered part of the old shopping centre. On the right is the luxurious Regent Cinema, a great favourite, with a True-Form shoe shop and Garlick and Sons, outfitters, to the right.

St Mary-le-Port church and grounds. All but the tower were destroyed in the war.

Two windows full of hats, from homburgs to boaters, put this branch of Dunn's in Mary-le-Port Street firmly in the pre-war years.

Mary-le-Port Street with the tower of St Mary church in the background. Shops in view include the Wholesale Drapery Warehouse to the left, Close and Company in front, and The Corner Shop to the right.

Tower Hill in the days when shops lined both sides of the streets and trams ran down the centre. Familiar names included Blakes Medical Stores, Veals' gunshop and cutlers, and Poeton's electro-plating works. The Prince of Wales pub sold Rogers Bristol Beers, made just a few yards away.

Another of Bristol's best-known shops in the 1930s, the Scholastic on the corner of High Street and Bridge Street.

Another picture of old Mary-le-Port Street, with Mrs E. Haynes' umbrella repair shop on the left, with Campbell's wallpaper shop beyond.

S. Veals and Sons in Tower Hill, then a gunshop and cutlers but better known since the war as a fishing tackle dealer. The company is now based in Old Market, a few hundred yards from the Tower Hill site which is now occupied by offices.

An unusual view of the Dutch House on the corner of Wine Street and High Street. Another famous Bristol building lost in the war.

Bristol Theatre Royal in King Street after houses were demolished to give it a street frontage but before it took over the Cooper's Hall on the right as an entrance hall and reception area. This frontage was demolished and rebuilt in the 1960s.

The construction of Sir Giles Gilbert Scott's much praised Electricity House at the end of The Centre in the late 1930s. The ship-shaped building, now insurance offices, was used during the war for the construction of Centaurus aircraft engines and its design was echoed in the new Lewis's department store in the Horsefair.

Practising for war on the anti-aircraft guns on board the *Flying Fox* training ship at Hotwells.

A memorable pair of pictures of Dump Harris, a famous Bristol comedian of his time and an acclaimed Oliver Hardy imitator. When Laurel and Hardy came to Bristol, Dump and his partner Freddy Godfrey were in the crowd to meet them, dressed as their heroes. The crowd loved it – Laurel and Hardy weren't amused.

The working Corn Exchange in the days before it became part of the St Nicholas Market complex.

The Official Proclamation in 1937 of the accession of King George VI to the throne. The Lord Mayor had to tour the city in a curious device apparently based on a pantomime coach, reading the notice to the assembled crowds. Top shows him outside the old Council House in Corn Street. *Middle left* shows the same scene from Broad Street with the Dutch House in the background. Middle centre shows the declaration at the junction of Union Street and The Horsefair, and *middle right* the ceremonial gun salute. Bottom is the Lord Mayor, coach and ceremonial police guard complete with maces.

A lorry from Pye Transport of London delivers newsprint to the *Evening Post* in Silver Street.

Newspaper delivery vans and cars line up outside the *Evening Post* offices in Silver Street, anxious to get the edition on the streets before the rival *Evening World*.

The remains of the old water mill at Winterbourne.

The New Inn on Bath Road, home of a pre-war benevolent society with a judge, ushers and clerk of the court which tried and fined regulars for a wide range of misdemeanours. The pub no longer exists.

George's delivery lorries, with 'Beer Is Best' written on the radiators, prepare to leave the brewery to take supplies to pubs across the city.

Some of the earliest motorised transport which gradually replaced the much-loved dray horses at George's Bristol brewery. This photograph comes from the early 1920s.

The old railway inn at Willsbridge, not far from the former LMS line from Bristol to Bath.

The famous Bristol Football Club 1920-21 team in the year the club moved to the Memorial Ground in Filton Avenue. These were the days when the club was one of the strongest on Britain and attracted huge crowds. The team included captain Reg Pickles with the ball, and internationals Len Corbett (seated fourth from left) and Sam Tucker (back row of players, fourth from left).

Bristol rugby hero Sam Tucker (known as 'Our Sam') was such a mighty figure in the game and so popular that he was honoured with his own orange wrapper. It was in use from the 1920s through to the 1960s, yet, because he was an amateur, he never received a penny in royalties.

Caricatures of Bristol Football Club in the 1920s. Our Sam – Sam Tucker – was there, of course; so is Tom Brown who was later banned from rugby for life after being found guilty of an alleged association with professional Rugby League.

Clifton Rugby Club, the pioneers of rugby tours, posing with a Fry's Chocolate-chartered plane at Whitchurch airfield.

A studio portrait of Len Corbett, arguably the greatest player ever to appear for Bristol Football Club. He captained England but was refused time off from his job at Fry's chocolate factory to tour South Africa with the British Isles team.

The captain of a visiting rugby team hanging a wreath on the gates of the Memorial Ground in an annual ceremony to remember the dead of World War One.

One of the big passenger liners that used to link Avonmouth with Canada, American and Australasia.

Bristol theatre favourites Peggy Ann Wood and Ronald Russell on their wedding day at Caxton Hall in London. They ran the Rapier Players at Bristol's Little Theatre for many years as part of two long and distinguished careers.

Victoria Street

The Tollgate

Part of a highly popular series of drawings of old Bristol by F.G.Lewin which appeared in 1922. Some of the detail may have been informed guesses but the drawings were praised for their historical accuracy. Also on following three pages.

Avon Gorge

Quaker's Friars

Right: Bomb damage in historic St Michael's Hill.

Above: The offices of the Gloucestershire regiment in St Michael's Hill the day after a bombing raid.

Below: A rescue worker digs deep into the ruins of a house in St Michael's Hill.

Two civil defence workers pause for a chat while clearing the remains of St Michael the Archangel (St Michael-On-The-Mount-Without) on St Michael's Hill.

Right, upper and lower: Dazed Bristolians walk through the ruins of Bristol's finest shopping area, Park Street.

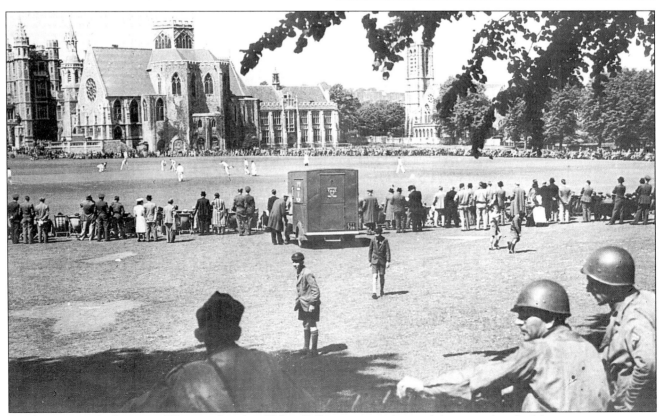

A quiet moment in the war as US troops based at Clifton College try to understand the mysteries of cricket.

Left: Clifton College Boys helping to move their library during the war. The school was evacuated to Bude in 1941 and the buildings occupied by American troops the following year.

Above: The South West Region War Council in a secret operations room in cellars below 19-21 Woodland Road, Clifton. The picture includes Mr H.M.Webb, City Engineer and ARP controller; George Gibbs, Lord Mayor's secretary; General Sir Hugh Elles, Regional Controller; a military adviser and Alderman F.A.Parish.

Two sailors take advantage of a quiet spring day at Snuff Mills.

Gassing over the garden fence. There may be a threat of air raids but even a gas mask can't stop a good gossip.

A victim of the Blitz in what was only described as 'a West town' rescues his few remaining belongings.

Above and left: Dramatic pictures of the end of one of the great granaries that were once a feature of the city docks.

American soldiers parade on College Green.

A classic image of the indomitable British spirit of the kind which the censors loved. Her home might have been blown apart but there's still time to reflect on the injustices of life with a quiet cigarette in the ruins.

An American GI and his Bristol girlfriend are interviewed by a BBC roving reporter on The Centre outside the Hippodrome.

Children take a break from the bombing at one of the country camps set up for war-weary Bristol families.

Bristol people take a close look at two of the planes that had been attacking the city. They were on display on The Centre to boost morale.

All that remained of Bedminster tram depot after an air raid.

Public transport in Bedminster came to a jarring halt after bombs demolished this tram in West Street in 1941.

Even the Blitz wasn't going to stop these Bedminster residents enjoying their Christmas party in an air raid shelter.

Bristol Fire Brigade pose with American GIs before the Yanks went home in 1945.

Blitz victims being fed at a parish hall somewhere in 'a West town' – usually a reference to Bristol.

Sailors help bombed-out Bristolians collect their remaining belongings.

The sad remains of a household somewhere in the city.

A new toy. Children competed with each other to find pieces of bomb casing and shrapnel from anti-aircraft guns, but these three seem to have a complete incendiary bomb that failed to ignite – a real prize.

The front of Temple Meads station is boarded up after it was damaged in a bombing raid.

Bristol Blitz victims get an unusual break in the oak panelled dining room of an Oxford college. They are at the table on the left – behind them are undergraduates.

War comes to the suburbs. This was once quiet Cheriton Place, between Westbury-on-Trym and Henleaze, which was bombed in April 1941.

Families who were bombed out had to make do with tents, although this toddler probably enjoyed the adventure of an open air bath.

Hats off to a party thrown for servicemen by the WVS in St David's Hall, Beauley Road, Southville.

The great adventure. Child evacuees from Bristol wait with their luggage on a country station for a train to safety.

A group of carefully tagged children and one battered teddy bear await evacuation at Temple Meads station.

A fake casualty for once as girls at Fairfield Grammar School are taught first aid by Red Cross workers in 1943.

The remains of shops in St James Barton in 1940. The pillars of the Upper Arcade can be seen to the right, while the wall next door belonged to Alsop's furniture shop. The van is from the Ministry of Information

The sad remnants of Bristol's Upper Arcade, opened in 1825, in the wake of a 1940 raid. It was one of two matching arcades, of which one still survives.

Land Army girls hoeing crops on a farm near Bristol. Second from right is Betty Lee, of Warden Road, Bedminster, a 20-year-old machinist at Wills tobacco factory.

Winston Churchill tours bomb-battered Bristol with his wife, Clementine, Bristol's Chief Constable Sir Charles Maby, American ambassador Mr J.G.Wynant who was in Bristol to get an honorary degree and General Sir Hugh Elles, South West Regional Controller.

A scene of utter devastation in Stafford Street, Bedminster, after a bombing raid in January 1941.

One of the most enduring images of World War Two in Bristol. It was January 1941, and it was so cold that water froze in the hosepipes while tea delivered by the WVS was iced up.

An evocative shot of Avonmouth docks in the post-war years. The ship in the centre is the *Manzanare* and to the right is the *Camito*, both registered in Glasgow. The tug to the left is the *Merrimac*.

The arrival of the first bananas at Avonmouth after the war was an occasion for civic rejoicing. The Home Secretary even went on the wireless to tell children who had never seen one how to open and eat it. This girl seems to have got the right idea.

An unknown ship is towed through the lock at Avonmouth by a tug.

Another unknown ship, high and dry in the graving dock at Avonmouth.

All that was left of Redcliffe Way after the war. Chatterton's house had amazingly survived, as had the Grosvenor Hotel in the background. This picture was taken from the grounds of St Mary Redcliffe church.

Another picture of Redcliffe Way, looking towards the bascule bridge. The WCA warehouse survives today as luxury flats, while the attractive red brick Co-op building below is now offices with a roundabout in front.

The Chatterton memorial outside St Mary Redcliffe Church, with the WCA warehouse (now flats) in the background. The memorial was never properly maintained and crumbled away until it was finally demolished in 1967.

The launch of the Juno from Charles Hill's Albion shipyard. Such launches were once a familiar sight in the Floating Harbour until its closure in 1976.

The Brabazon under construction in its enormous purpose-built assembly hall with its great glass wall. Notice the huge propellers in the foreground and the amazing height of the tailplane.

The naming ceremony for the ill-fated Brabazon, a giant of the skies intended to be Britain's main contender on the transatlantic air run. Only two were built and both were scrapped. This is the first, outside the gigantic specially built assembly hall at Filton and still without its enormous wings or tailplane.

More photographs from the naming ceremony for the Brabazon.

The Brabazon dwarfs its ground crew as it is wheeled out for its maiden flight in 1949. The picture shows the sheer size of its assembly hall with one wall made from glass.

The Brabazon silhouetted against the clouds on one of its few flights.

The Brabazon on one of the test flights before it was decided to scrap the project.

A rare photograph of two Brabazons, together in the vast assembly hall at Filton. They were out of date before even one flew, and both were scrapped in 1953.

Excavations of the remains of the old Bristol Castle in 1948. The enormous castle, second only to the Tower of London, was destroyed after the Civil War and all the remaining foundations have now been uncovered and put on display.

Above right and below: Winston Churchill, Chancellor of Bristol University, arrives at Filton airfield for a visit to the city.

Rysbrack's famous statue of William III being returned to Queen Square. It was kept at Badminton House for safety during the war.

Excavation of a Roman villa at Lawrence Weston in 1947. It is believed to have been the home of a rich Romanised Briton from around 270AD and was entered through an impressive portico with six columns of Bath stone and a columned porch. The remains show signs of having been attacked and burned by raiders.

Crowds at Temple Meads station boarding a Paddington express. Notice the destination boards on the carriages, and the overhead signs to the telegraph and advertising Bowyers Bath sausages.

Medieval times return to Christmas Steps, even if it was just for a press call. The original caption has been lost but these are probably local amdrammers publicising a new show. Notice the bulky cameras and tripod needed in the days of slow film.

Post war Wine Street before it was rebuilt. The side to the right is now offices: that to the left is now Castle Park, Lloyds Bank and the former Bank of England building.

All that remained of Bristol's second Colston Hall after it burned down in February 1945. Ironically, the first hall had also burned down, in 1898. The third hall (the present one) opened in 1951 as part of the Festival of Britain celebrations.

The bombed remains of Castle School, Castle Green. It stood where the mound and children's playground are now in Castle Park.

Labour hero and Health Minister Nye Bevan laying the foundation stone of a council house in Arnell Drive, Henbury, in the late 1940s.

Dennis Roberts, a giant centre-half, who played in more than 500 matches for Bristol City in the 1930s and 1940s.

The New Zealand Expeditionary Forces XV attracted a full house to the Memorial Ground just after the war. Charlie Murphy, a well-known Bristol player, is second from left.

Ray Warren, arguably the best captain Bristol Rovers ever had. He played for the club from 1935-36 to 1955-56 and also guested for Bristol City, Bath City and Leeds United. He retired to run a pub and died in 1988.

Evening Post 1947

The height of modern technology – a teleprinter. This replaced the morse code machine and was eventually itself replaced by computer links.

The wire room, the heart of the *Evening Post*'s out-of-Bristol news service. District offices and national news services were linked to the paper here.

The stone where slugs of type were made up into pages in a process which had hardly changed for centuries.

The huge reels of newsprint on the presses.

Papers being packed in the publishing department to be sent all over the world.

A smartly-dressed newspaper seller – smarter than his customer in fact – at work on The Centre, not far from the offices of the rival *Evening World*.

One of the amazing Linotype machines where hot metal was transformed into slugs of type with the aid of some of the fastest keyboard operators in the business. The noise and smell of Linotypes added to the excitement of newspaper production.

The Lanson tube delivery system, once a familiar sight in shops as well as offices. Copy or messages were placed in glass tubes and driven by compressed air around the building. It was not unknown for the odd mouse to pop out with the carrier.

Maintenance workers on the Suspension Bridge chains, high above the Avon.

A new road bridge being built to carry Union Street across Fairfax Street. Fairfax House department store was later built on land to the right.

Union Street as it was before the Galleries Shopping Centre replaced the shops on the right. Businesses there then included Harrolds' fashion shop, opticians Pictons, and Fry's Baby Fayre.

The Baptist Church in Old King Street (now Merchant Street) stands amid the desolation of war.

The Hart and Co smithy in Old King Street when the business had been adapted to specialise in vehicle springs.

Merchant Street (formerly Old King Street, as the street sign states) fallen on hard times. T.Deas and Sons, wholesale clothiers, later relocated to Wilder Street. Neighbouring businesses included Rouch and Penny, electrical engineers and contractors, Fair Deal cash registers and Henry Matthews and Co.

Work on the long task to rebuilding war damaged Bristol. This is the corner of Old King Street and what was Castle Mill Street, with The Clock Shop next to the Old King Street chapel. Fry's chocolate factory chimney stands tall in the background.

This beautiful early 18th-century house in Old King Street was home to the city Weights and Measures Department in the 1950s. Since then, it has been a bank and pub among other uses.

Another view of Old King Street. All that survives from this scene are the ornate gate and railings on the right and the listed building behind which is now a pub. Businesses included T.Deas and Sons, wholesale clothiers, Henry Matthews and Co, and electrical contractors Rouch and Penny, and patent flourmillers H.Jones ('Towers Above Them All').

The Baptist Church in Old King Street.

The rebuilding of Old King Street as Merchant Street.

College Green after the war. The Civic Restaurant which tried to serve decent meals by austerity standards is to the right.

The old bridge which carried the Docks Railway across the entrance to Bathurst Basin after it emerged from a tunnel beneath Redcliffe. It lifted to allow boats to pass through.

A sunny lunch time on College Green with the lawns filled with sun-bathing office workers.

The lowering of College Green in 1950. The walls were removed, as were thousands of tons of earth and an admired row of trees was cut down. The building to the left of the cathedral is the Royal Hotel which has since been expanded and refurbished as the Swallow Royal.

How are the mighty brought low! These are vandal-damaged figures of kings and queens (all of whom gave Bristol various charters) from Bristol's replica High Cross on College Green. They are James I, Elizabeth I, Henry VI and Charles I, and they were taken down in 1950 during the lowering of College Green. Part of the cross was rebuilt in Berkeley Square, Clifton, in 1956.

Bristol's new Council House under construction on College Green.

The original *Evening Post* head office in Silver Street where the newspaper all Bristol asked for and helped to create was born.

Evening Post 1950s

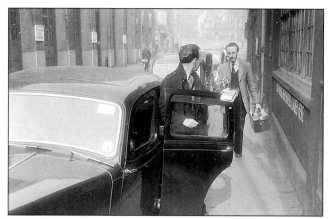

A reporter and photographer dashing off on a story.

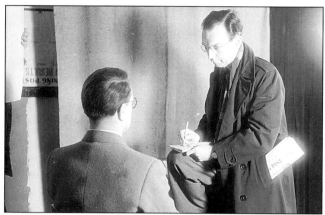

Our ace reporter questions an informant.

Our reporter highlights how up-to-date the paper was as he phones his story from the car.

A photographer, complete with standard snapper's hat and huge camera and flash, in the studio.

The Linotype operators who set sub-edited stories into metal type.

These curious machines are teletypes, bringing and sending news from all over the world via phone and land lines.

The stone where type, advertisements, headings and picture blocks were made into pages.

The presses roll and the first papers are printed.

The head office of the *Western Daily Press*, Bristol's oldest surviving newspaper, in Baldwin Street. Small ads cost just 3d a word then.

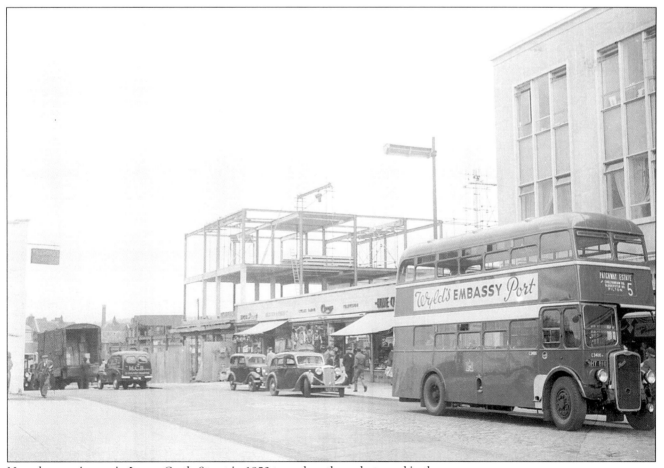

New shops going up in Lower Castle Street in 1953 to replace those destroyed in the war.

The desolation left well into the 1950s in the Castle Street area. The white building in the centre background is the new Lewis' store, and Fry's chocolate factory chimney survives to the left.

The Rising Sun pub in Lower Castle Street in the early 1950s.

The University Settlement in Ducie Road, Barton Hill. It was set up by Bristol University in 1911 to appease middle class consciences about the plight of the working classes, and even ran a soup kitchen for striking Great Western Cotton factory workers. It is now a community centre.

The Great Western Cotton factory in Barton Hill, once one of the area's major employers. It closed in 1925 during the recession. The buildings were demolished in 1968.

Maze Street in the heart of old Barton Hill before the redevelopers moved in.

New blocks of flats – Bristol's first and the tallest outside London – going up in Barton Hill after a massive slum clearance programme. High rise living was then seen as the answer to rehousing families.

The bleak outpatients' department at the Bristol Royal Infirmary in the early days of the NHS.

The White Funnel paddle steamer *Glen Usk* aground on a bend on the Avon like so many ships before her.

The *Glen Usk*, photographed from the Zig Zag Path from Clifton to Portway.

The White Funnel paddle steamer *Glen Gower* in Cumberland Basin.

Bristol City's hallowed turf being replaced. The stand behind was replaced by the current Dolman stand (named after a former chairman) in the 1960s, as were the floodlights.

The naval reserve training ship *Flying Fox* actually going somewhere instead of being permanently moored at Hotwells as most people remember her. To the left is the Bush warehouse which later became the Arnolfini arts centre.

The much missed Little Theatre, built in a small hall at the front of the main Colston Hall. Many big names appeared there in the days when it was run as a second venue by Bristol Old Vic, but it was eventually converted into a bar for the Colston Hall.

Rural Lawrence Weston before a huge council estate took over the area.

Hotwell Road which still looks much the same, more than half a century after the war. There has been some tidying up and new building, and the railway line along the docks has gone, but the road remains an eyesore.

Part of the wonderful Winter Garden at Ashton Court, one of the features created by the Smyth family in Victorian times.

Above and below: Col R.N.Harrison's house, St James's Barton, before it was demolished for road widening. It was a fine Georgian mansion, built around 1728 and once considered for the official residence of the Mayor of Bristol. It was demolished in the face of many protests in 1960.

St James's Barton before redevelopment. Businesses advertising at the end of the old houses include steamship agents Stewart and Esplen and freight shippers Neale and Wilkinson.

The dereliction that German bombers left of St James's Barton.

King Square, looking towards Jamaica Street and Stokes Croft behind and looking very unloved. This is long before it was beautifully restored.

King Square, at its dullest as a municipal park surrounded by businesses. The Tudor Rose transport hotel is featured *above* and the best-known company, gear specialists Llewellin Machine Company, *below,* with the Tudor Rose to the left of the empty site.

King Street before it became part of Bristol's leisure area. The tall building on the right later became Renatos' famed theatre restaurant, La Taverna Dell' Artista, a haunt of the famous for 50 years.

Redcliff Hill, with the Redcliff Salon offering hair dyeing, tinting and permanent waving. To the left of the salon is Brown's gardening shop, now located in Bridewell.

The new flats at Redcliffe going up to rehouse people displaced by the war, road widening and slum clearance.

The demolition of the old Broadmead Post Office in 1951.

Left: Broadmead Baptist Chapel, opened in 1640 and one of the oldest in Britain. It was demolished to make way for shops with a new chapel on the upper floor.

Another view of post-war Wine Street after the ruins of war had been cleared and the area was being used as a car park.

A scene that never was. This is Wine Street, complete with grass and grazing sheep and a horse. This famous practical joke – put together long before computer manipulation made such reality altering easy – was a satirical comment on what might happen if Bristol's rates went any higher.

Happy crowds at *(left)* a Bristol City v Brighton match and *(right)* a Bristol Rovers v Luton game.

Happy family football crowds in a gentler sporting era. *Middle left* was taken at the famous Bristol Rovers v Newcastle Cup-tie in 1951 for which Bristol virtually closed down. Some 40,000 people got tickets and enough people to fill the ground three times over were turned away. Newcastle won and went on to win the Cup. *Middle right* shows avid Robin (Bristol City) supporters at a match against Birmingham. *Above* features a local derby between the two Bristol clubs.

Milk Street, swept away in new road developments with only the Lamb and Flag pub still in business. In the distance is Dunn's menswear shop and the new Jones' store going up in The Horsefair.

Milk Street again with the Crown and Cushion pub to the left. Cherry Alley runs to the right next to Leigh Gay's part exchange shop.

Another view of Milk Street with the cafe name curiously spelled in the American way. There was an interesting bow fronted shop to the left.

All the pictures on this page are of Kingweston House, Vanbrugh's great mansion overlooking the Severn and the Welsh coast (and industrial Avonmouth these days), and its lovely gardens before it fell on hard times. It is now owned by the city council which is seeking a suitable use for it.

The lily pond in the walled garden at Kingweston House, for a long time a favourite leisure area for Bristolians.

One of the old bucket dredgers which used to keep the floating harbour and river clear of mud.

A 14th-century arch at Quakers Friars, hardly enhanced by the modern building next door, and demolished in the mid-1950s.

The last meeting in the old Council House in Corn Street before the city council moved to College Green in 1956. The building is now used for a Crown Court.

No 12 College Street (formerly No 69 but renumbered) where cinematography pioneer William Friese-Greene was born in 1855. What is now Brunel House (a hotel built by Brunel for his rail and sea service from London to America) can be seen to the right.

A view of The Horsefair with Union Street beyond and Lewis' new store to the left. The huge chimney of Fry's old chocolate factory still dominates the scene to the right.

The Haymarket and Horsefair before Lewis' store was built on the big open site in the background. Notice the ornate cast-iron railings marking the underground public conveniences on the traffic island.

Views of The Horsefair area in the years between the war and the redevelopment of the new Broadmead shopping centre.

The Carpenter's Arms in The Horsefair, with a typewriter maintenance and service shop to the right and Urch's flower service to the left. All these lovely old buildings disappeared to road building and redevelopment.

Another view of the car park which took over Bristol's bombed shopping centre for many years. To the left is the shell of St Peter's Church, with the towers and spires of St Nicholas, St Mary-le-Port, All Saints', St Stephen's and Christ Church behind.

Site works for the new Lewis' store with the Haymarket entrance to Marks and Spencer's Broadmead store on the left.

The famous Lewis' department store, with its shiplike prow, going up on the corner of Horsefair, with the new Jones' store framework behind. Lewis's was later taken over by John Lewis (no relation) and, most recently, Bentalls, while Jones' became Debenhams.

The elegant Lewis' store under construction. The curved design echoed that of the much praised Electricity House on The Centre.

Another part of Bristol swept away after the war. The Crown and Cushion pub sits on the end of St James's Square Avenue, with Shopfittings (Bristol); F.Mitchell and Sons, scrap merchants; Leigh Gay, and Cleaves Store to the right.

The Kingstonian, once a familiar sight touring the city harbour and River Avon. The passengers in this photograph are all young men with similar clothes and haircuts – students or apprentices perhaps?

A master and students at Clifton College walk past the statue of old boy Earl Haig whose leadership in World War One led to the slaughter of so many other Clifton boys.

The harbourmaster's house, complete with clock tower which sat alongside the lock entrance at Cumberland Basin. It was used as a base by the builders of the flyover bridge, then demolished in 1964.

The Cumberland Basin end of the Floating Harbour when it was still a working docks. On the left is the old pump house which is now a popular pub, while houses have replaced the dockside buildings beyond and across the water.

Westbury-on-Trym on a quiet day in the 1950s, when J.H.Mills was selling Doone Valley Butter, Westbury Radio was a Bush dealer, and R.J.Tutton stocked Bond Street Shoes.

Tugs pull a coaster into Avonmouth docks past the swing bridge. The number of cranes is evidence of the level of business the docks were attracting.

The little tug Medway sails past the timber ship *Plancius* in the Floating Harbour.

The tug *Cabot* sailing past ships unloading in the Floating Harbour in the days when it was a busy working port. The tower of the cathedral can just be glimpsed behind the sheds.

A pleasure cruise around the harbour which was still a working port then. The boat was photographed by the bascule bridge at Redcliffe, with the WCA building looming in the background.

Big crowds at the Memorial Ground watch Bristol score against Bath in 1951.

Fred Morgan's furniture shop in Merchant Street. Little of this scene survives today.

The remains of the George Adlam and Sons' brass and iron foundry, between Narrow Weir and Ellbroad Street. They made brewing equipment but had moved the factory to Fishponds by this time, keeping only offices on this site.

Views of the city in the 1950s from St Mary Redcliffe church. *Middle left* shows houses in old Redcliffe behind the church, with new flats behind. *Middle right* shows a long vanished railway goods yard at the side of the church with the line from Temple Meads to the Floating Harbour to the right and a glassworks and cone just visible beyond. *Bottom left* shows old riverside warehouses and mills now turned into flats, with the bascule bridge to the left. *Bottom right* shows the General Hospital behind the houses of Redcliffe Hill, with the John Robinson factory to the right and children lined up in the school playground to the left. The castle-like building in the lower left is the top of the famous Shot Tower, demolished in 1968 for road widening.

An unusual weather vane of a lamp-lighter, carrying the tools of his trade, in Avon Street.

The new Bristol airport at Lulsgate, which took over from Whitchurch in 1957, with Cambrian Airline planes.

Whitchurch airport, opened in 1930, and once planned as a major international crossroads. Although it played an important role in World War Two, the city bought the better-placed Lulsgate airfield and Whitchurch closed in 1957.

A quiet moment in Somerset Square, Redcliffe with a mystery Georgian monument in the middle. The tall flats around the modern square had yet to be built.

Winston Churchill on one of his regular visits to Bristol as Chancellor of the University. *pictured left* shows him at Temple Meads Station and *right* unveiling a plaque in 1954.

Winston Churchill in his ceremonial robes as Chancellor of Bristol University.

The interior of the Empire Theatre where Cary Grant had his first show business job as a limelighter. The theatre was a music hall, BBC studios and popular amdram venue before it was swept away in the early 1960s to make way for the inner circuit road.

Haile Selassi, Emperor of Abyssinia (Ethiopia) who fled to Britain when his country was invaded by the Italians. He lived in Bath for a while and was a familiar sight in the area. *Left* shows him inspecting an honour guard of Bristol war veterans. Below he is touring the Bristol Aeroplane Company factory at Filton.

Maggs' famous store in Queen's Road, Clifton. The empty site next door was a part of the terrace that had been bombed and has since been replaced.

Above: Three photographs from Harry Stoke drift mine near Bristol, opened in 1954 and closed in 1963. The coal mined was used to produce gas and electricity for Bristol but the pit was never profitable. The 220 miners transferred to Norton Hill and other Somerset pits.

Bristol University's new engineering faculty towers over the houses of Woodland Road. The more traditional university and museum buildings in Queen's Road cluster around the tower of the Wills Memorial Building, with Berkeley Square in the foreground.

The building of the dam across the Chew Valley to form a reservoir to supply Bristol. The medieval hamlet of Stratford was drowned when the lake filled up.

Left and below: Stratford Mill on Blaise estate. This was an 18th-century corn grinding mill from the village of Stratford which was drowned beneath Chew Valley reservoir in the 1950s. The mill was rebuilt next to Hazel Brook in 1954.

The Empress Queen moored in St Augustine's Reach.

The peaceful haven of St James's Park, off The Horsefair.

The remains of Bristol Castle gateway surrounded by the dereliction of war. The building was later restored and used for a restaurant among other things. The tower of St Peter's Church is in the background to the left, across what is now Castle Park.

Bristol's acclaimed shopping centre after the war – transformed into a car park. On the right is the shell of Jones and Co's furniture shop in Mary-le-Port Street and St Mary-le-Port church, with St Peter's Church in the background.

Park Street, looking less than its usually elegant self. The ruins of the bombed shops have been cleared but the terrace of shops had yet to be restored. Even so, it was business in temporary premises.

The Wills memorial Building in Queen's Road, floodlit for the Queen's coronation in 1953.

Midland Region loco No.40174 pulls a train into St Philip's station.

St Philip's station, opened in 1870 to relieve pressure on the main LMS terminus at Temple Meads. Passenger services ended in 1953 and the neighbouring goods yard closed in 1967.

Passengers crowd on to a train at Temple Meads in the days before every family had a car. The battered suitcases everywhere reflect the post-war austerity of the early 1950s.

One of the stylised sea horses and riders commissioned for Bristol's new Council House which was opened by the Queen on College Green in 1956. It replaced the Old Council House in Corn Street which is now a Crown Court.

The tug *Danegarth* in Avonmouth docks. On the right is the banana boat *Bayano*.

The Lord Mayor of Bristol touring the city in the bizarre Proclamation Coach, heading a ceremonial procession to formally announcing the coronation of the Queen in 1953.

Part of a rare series of pictures showing life inside Horfield prison in the days when access was rarely granted to the cameras. Left shows the bakery where warders wore white coats. Below left are the galleries of cells, and below right is the chapel exterior and interior.

A spectacular shot *(left)* of the biggest-ever fire in the Bristol area when six oil storage tanks caught fire at Avonmouth in 1951. Sixty-five fire appliances attended from as far away as Wolverhampton.

Navel ratings helping fight the fire take a tea-break.

Festival of Britain celebrations in Bristol in 1951. *Above and below* are some of the street decorations on The Centre and Queen Square.

A bizarre meeting between the Dagenham Girl Pipers in full Scottish outfits and Tanganyikan tribal dignitaries at the Our Way of Life exhibition.

A Civil War re-enactment as part of a pageant on the Downs.

The special decorations on the front of Temple Meads station

The banner on Bristol Bridge with the Robinson building to the right and war battered Victoria Street behind.

Another picture of the building of the dam which was to bottle up the River Chew and turn a pleasant valley into a huge lake to provide water for Bristol.

Red Maids School, an 18th-century building in Denmark Street which the school took over in 1723. It was rebuilt in 1843. The school moved out in 1911, and the building became government offices. It was demolished and replaced in 1952 by Bristol's first high rise office block. Shops to the left include Whitefield, Hodgeson and Brough, and Speedy Shoe Service.

Firemen among the wreckage of a Vampire jet which crashed into Avon Gorge after the pilot, Flying Officer John Crossley from Filton-based 501 Squadron, flew beneath Clifton Suspension Bridge in 1957. It was an illegal flight to protest against the disbandment of the squadron.

A roadside memorial to the soldiers of the Gloucestershire Regiment who died in the Korean War.

Terraced houses at the back of the huge Wills tobacco factory in Bedminster. The entire economy of Bedminster and Southville was once based on the factory and its hundreds of workers.

The remains of Rennison's Baths at Montpelier, once part of a famous Victorian pleasure gardens. It was then outside the city boundary so not bound by licensing laws, and was a favourite outing for Bristolians. Part of the gardens survive in the grounds of neighbouring Colston's Girls' School but this building was demolished to make way for Montpelier Health Centre.

Baldwin Street in the late 1950s or early 1960s when the fruit and vegetable market was still there and the road was still quiet enough to unload lorries parked at right angle to the pavement.

An Anderson shelter from the war, converted into a garden shed to serve one of the new prefabs which housed hundreds of people who lost their homes to bombing raids and post-war redevelopment.

Staff at the Imperial Sports Ground in 1955. The ground, off West Town Lane, was one of the best in Britain and host to numerous international sporting events.

Bedminster Cricket Club First XI, photographed on their ground at The Clannage, Ashton, in 1952 with Avon Gorge and the Suspension Bridge in the background.

A quiet study of veteran Bristol theatre couple Peggy Ann Wood and Ronald Russell. The couple ran the Rapier Players at the Little Theatre for many years.

A tall funnelled ship is towed by tug into Avonmouth docks.

Stevedores unloading a timber ship at Avonmouth.

High and dry in the dry dock at Avonmouth.

Bristol Rovers star Geoff Bradford in balletic pose at Eastville stadium in the 1950s. Behind him is the south stand which later burned down.

Three great Rovers' players. *Left to right:* The tragic Harry Bamford, an elegant gentlemanly player, who was killed in 1958 in a motorcycle accident at the age of 38. More than 35,000 people packed Eastville Stadium for a benefit match for his family between a combined Rovers and City side and Arsenal. Alfie Biggs one of the greatest players ever to put on a Rovers shirt. Nicknamed The Baron for his snappy dress style, he might have played for England had he been with a bigger club but he was happy to stay at Eastville. Harold Jarman, the skilled winger who became Rovers' third top scorer after the main strikers. He also played football for New York Cosmos and cricket for Gloucestershire and stepped in as caretaker manager of Rovers in 1980.

The great John Atyeo, signed to Bristol City in 1951 on top wages of £12 a week. The team's finest post-war star and an England international player who brought eggs for his teammates from his chicken farm. He retired after 645 games to become a teacher.

A Christmas party at Southmead Youth Club in the 1950s.

Leaders and members of Southmead Youth Club in the 1950s.

The Sixties & Seventies

IF THE 1950s were a time for sowing seeds, the 1960s were the years of harvesting. It was a time for new buildings of unsurpassed ugliness which still blight the city today, for new roads which completed the damage to old communities caused by the war – and for the cult of the teenager.

Teenagers were invented in the 1950s but really came to power in the 1960s. And this new generation of youngsters with money, ambition, and their own form of entertainment changed the city as rapidly as the new speculative offices springing up everywhere.

The 1960s also saw a renaissance of the arts in Bristol, the like of which has not been seen since, apart from the dance music explosion of the 1990s.

Among those working in the city were playwrights Tom Stoppard, Peter Nichols, John Arden and Charles Wood; film-makers John Boorman and Michael Croucher; novelists Angela Carter and Terry Pratchett; director/writers John Hale and Geoffrey Reeves; artists David Inshaw, Derek Balmer, Alf Stockham, Neil Murison, and Ernie Pascoe among many others; and chef and TV presenter Keith Floyd.

The city also boasted two nationally famous clubs – The Troubadour in Clifton (later immortalised in Al Stewart's song, *Clifton in the Rain*) and the Blues Club at the Full Moon, Stokes Croft, one of the two responsible for the blues revival in Britain. More big names appeared at those two clubs and the then world class Bristol Old Vic than can be listed here.

It was also a decade that saw music hall star George Formby and new rock sensations The Beatles appearing in Bristol, together with new American style ranch homes with fitted kitchens, BBC2, *Coronation Street*, and Uncle Bonny's Chinese Jazz Club ('Chop Chop Velly Good') at the Corn Exchange.

A movie called *Some People* (Angela Douglas, Kenneth More, David Hemmings) was filmed in the city and introduced the world to the justly famed Magnet fish and chip bar in Bedminster.

Mini skirts filled the streets, and mods and rockers turned Bank Holidays into battlefields at Weston-super-Mare. The New Entertainment Centre – widescreen cinema, Locarno ballroom, Silver Blades ice rink – opened in Frogmore Street, and old military gear and ancient fur coats were *de rigeur* in the clubs.

Devastating floods ravaged much of the city and surrounding towns and the central shopping area of Broadmead was heading for pedestrianisation. And down the road at Shepton Mallet, the predecessor of the great Glastonbury festivals was launched with Pink Floyd, The Byrds, Jefferson Airplane, Fleetwood Mac, Donovan, Fairport Convention and Led Zeppelin on the bill.

The 1970s opened with venues like the Bamboo Club in St Paul's (an early venture by long distance yachtsman Tony Bullimore), and The Granary, the Mandrake, Caesar's and numerous strip clubs.

Concorde was the pride and hope of Bristol but never caught on, while Bristol jammed solid every summer as the M5 reached Avonmouth then decanted holiday traffic through the city while the river was being bridged.

The first Severn Bridge and the M32 – The Parkway – cut travelling times to the rest of the country, while the city and county of Bristol was swallowed up – albeit temporarily – in the new Avon county.

After the floods of the 1960s, there were the droughts of the 1970s and the country's first-ever water rationing. There were even echoes of VE parties when whole streets closed to celebrate the Queen's Silver Jubilee.

By the time the 1980s came along, Bristol had changed in every way and far more dramatically than anyone could have dreamed in the dark days after the war. Here are some of the most enduring images of those years.

Bristol Stock Exchange in St Nicholas Street. It was founded in 1845 at the height of railway mania and moved to these premises in 1903. These were the days when prices varied from exchange to exchange so investors could make a fortune buying and selling between them. It closed in 1991 when business was transferred to Birmingham.

The old and the new. *Top left*, cars queue for one of the last Aust ferries to Beachley on the Welsh side as the Severn Bridge, which was soon to replace them, nears completion. *Top right* shows one of the famous ferries crossing the river, and in *middle left* cars waiting on the slipway for a ferry to dock. *Middle right* pictures a ferry on the slipway, and bottom the *Severn Queen*, slightly off its usual course and beneath the Suspension Bridge.

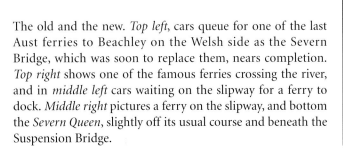

Miners at the Harry Stoke drift mine, part of the great Bristol coal field that stretched from Coalpit Heath to Radstock. It closed in 1963.

The RNR training ship *Flying Fox*, moored at Hotwells between 1922 and 1973 when she was broken up. The RNR moved to shore based headquarters in Winterstoke Road in 1972.

The original Shot Tower on Redcliff Hill where William Watts invented perfectly spherical lead shot after dreaming about a new process. It closed in 1968 for road widening and was demolished.

The Ashton rail bridge when this was still a full working waterside railway. Steam trains do still run down to here from the Industrial Museum on the enthusiast-run Bristol Harbour Railway.

Crossing the river, old style. This was the main route from Bristol to the south and west before the Cumberland Basin flyover was built.

This attractive river is usually a road in Ashton but the great flood of 1968 made a boat a more realistic prospect than a car.

Penn Street, just before the buildings at the right were torn down for a new stores and shops. The main building is the Whitefield Tabernacle.

The old Co-op building on The Centre. The clock was a rendezvous point for lovers and theatre-goers for generations, but this amazing gothic building couldn't be updated for modern needs and was replaced by a new one. *Left:* All of the attractive buildings to the left have also gone. *Above:* The entrance and a small wharf crane.

The Empire Theatre, Old Market, in its final days before it was demolished, with all the buildings to the left, for the Inner Circuit road. *Left* shows the exterior and *middle right* a view from the stalls. *Bottom left* is the stage door and *bottom right* the frontage when it was being used as a BBC studio. In the early days, before it had a drinks licence, audiences had to nip into the White Hart next door at intervals.

Old Market before it started coming up in the world. The Bunch of Grapes and the Don Cafe are now combined as The Old Market Tavern, Easiephit has long gone but Hurwood's pram shop is still there. The bomb site beyond was filled in with a very indifferent building that still spoils the restored street frontage.

Middle Terrace, Castle Green, a row of nine identical two-up, two-down houses with no electricity and water obtained from a pump in the back yard. This photograph was taken in 1960 but the terrace had changed little since the war. This area is now beneath Castle Park.

Evening Post in the 1960s

The *Evening Post* at Silver Street in the 1960s. The top two and bottom two show the reporters' room. Below is the news desk, the hub of the operation. Right are the copytakers who took down news stories over the phone, and below them the sub-editors who butcher beautifully-written prose (reporter's definition)/carefully hone and shape roughly-written copy into stories (sub-editor's definition).

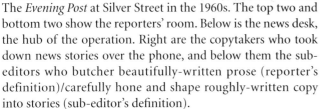

Enthusiasts discover the last resting place of an old Bristol tram, in a back garden at Almondsbury. Left, it is being loaded on to a lorry to be restored.

Left: The Mardyke ferry which once carried passengers across the Floating Harbour. Its route is now covered by the new ferries that serve the waterfront.

Standing outside the sheds that were to become Watershed, shops, bars and the GWR Radio studios and looking across to Narrow Quay and The Centre. The Bristol and West Building Society headquarters has yet to be built.

These three pictures show the sad end of St Augustine the Less, the little church in the shadow of Bristol Cathedral which was first bombed, then demolished to make way for the Swallow Royal extension. *Above:* The rubble-filled interior. *Middle:* Its fine position overlooking St Augustine's Reach. *Right:* The last vestiges of the roof with The Centre behind.

A wonderfully evocative picture of the bottom of Christmas Steps at night. Little has changed to the right of the road but the shops on the left have all be replaced by new offices.

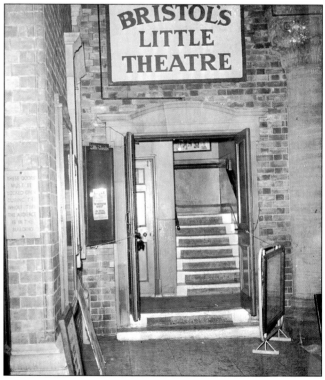

The days of the Rapier Players, run by Peggy Ann Wood and Ronald Russell at the Little Theatre in front of the Colston Hall. *Top left* shows the cramped backstage area with Peggy Ann second from right, holding what seems to be a spear. *Top right* demonstrates the problems of getting scenery flats into the building through the ancient cellars beneath, and above the tiny entrance. *Middle left* is a view of the cosy auditorium.

Children on the much-loved rock slide on The Downs where generations of little bottoms have polished the rock until it shines.

Bristol bridge with Victoria Street beyond. Top picture features two buildings with their tops lopped off by wartime bombing – the George's brewery offices to the left which have now been rebuilt from old photographs, and the Robinson headquarters to the right which has been replaced by a tower block. The riverside site to the right has also been filled in with offices. The picture below also includes part of Welsh Back with one of the many public conveniences surrounded by cast ironwork which once dotted the city.

Bristol Hippodrome when it was still crowned by a truncated spire and globe, and an extension to the left had not been built. The canopy over the front entrance has recently been recreated.

Scenes *above* from the regular greyhound racing at Knowle Stadium, which was demolished in 1961 to make way for new housing.

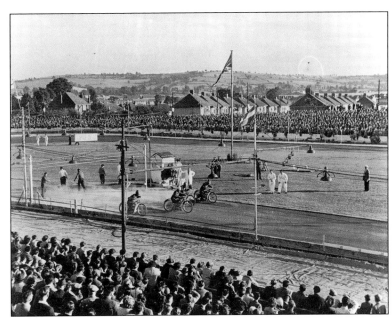

Two views of the speedway which shared the Knowle Stadium track with greyhounds and attracted huge crowds on Friday nights.

The demolition of a famous Bristol landmark, the 300ft chimney of the former Fry's factory near the Pithay in 1961. It was reduced to 80ft in height by steeplejacks before the rest was blown up.

The interior of Broadmead Baptist Church before it was demolished in 1967 and replaced with shops with a new chapel above.

This is the part of Canons Marsh which is now the Lloyds bank amphitheatre and headquarters. The huge white tobacco bonds were blown up in 1988, and the area cleared for redevelopment.

Scenes from Goram Fair, a much-loved annual jamboree on the Blaise estate. It was one of the most popular events held in the city and was revived in Avon Gorge in 1997 as part of the celebrations to mark the beginning of the Matthew's voyage to Newfoundland.

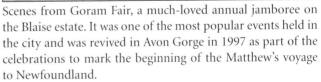

Pannier tank No.3650 pulls a docks railway train through the tunnel under Redcliffe and crosses the bridge across the entrance

thurst Basin which lifted to allow ships to enter. The General Hospital is on the right.

The MV *Angelo* leaves the Floating Harbour and heads downstream to the Bristol Channel. Ships as big as this had to judge the tides perfectly if they were to navigate the bends of the Avon without grounding.

Bedminster Bridge and Redcliffe Hill before it was made into a dual carriageway. The buildings on the right has been demolished.

The famous illuminated ceiling at the Locarno ballroom, Bristol's premiere 1960s dance venue in the new Bristol Centre.

Busy Welsh Back when it was still the city's main fruit and veg market. None of the offices which fill this frontage now had been built.

A gathering of Bristol Old Players' Society (rugby) at the Memorial Ground in the 1960s. Ace player Len Corbett, by then a rugby writer for a national paper, is seated fourth from left. Tom Mahoney, Bristol's secretary and past president, is standing third from left.

Bristol Rugby Club in the early 1970s when the club won the unofficial English/Welsh club championship. Players include captain Tony Nicholls with the ball, and England international David Rollitt (seated, far left).

Len Corbett, Bristol's finest rugby player, in his 80s at his cottage at Horner on Exmoor, not long before his death.

Alan Morley of Bristol (with the ball) who claimed a place in the *Guinness Book of Records* as the leading all time try scorer in world rugby. He made more than 500 appearances for the club from 1968 onwards.

A rare colour photograph of rock singer Eddie Cochran and his girlfriend, singer-songwriter Sharon Sheeley (although only shown here in black and white). It was taken in 1960, a few weeks before Cochran's final concert at Bristol Hippodrome. The following day, the car taking Sheeley, Cochran, and co-star Gene Vincent to Heathrow hit a lamppost at Chippenham after a tyre burst. Cochran died in St Martin's Hospital, Bath, and Sharon had back and leg injuries. She was visited in hospital by the Everly Brothers.

Most of the photographs in this book are available as high quality 5in x 7in prints and would make marvellous gifts when suitably framed.

How To Order

A photocopy of the picture you want would be most helpful, but please give:

1. The page number in this book
2. The position on the page (top right, lower left, etc.)
3. The first line of the caption
Prices are £4 each print, inclusive of postage and VAT.

Send your cheque, payable to Bristol Evening Post and Press, with your full address and daytime telephone number to:

PHOTOSALES,
Bristol Evening Post and Press Ltd,
Temple Way,
BRISTOL BS99 7HD

Orders can also be placed in our Temple Way offices, but telephone orders cannot be accepted.